Daily Vocabulary

LEVEL 3

THE FIVE MINUTE WORKOUT™

ML **McDougal, Littell & Company**

Evanston, Illinois

Dallas   Phoenix   Columbia, SC

Development assistance for *Daily Vocabulary* was provided by
Wordworks Publishing Services of Gloucester, Massachusetts.

ISBN 0-8123-8333-8

1 2 3 4 5 6 7 8 9 10 –WRW– 98 97 96 95 94

INTRODUCTION

Philosophy

Daily Vocabulary invites students to play with words and sense their magic. This program develops word power through a variety of daily activities. Brief, lively, and fun-to-do, these activities help make students curious about words and eager to explore their meanings.

Program Design

Daily Vocabulary consists of six teacher's manuals, one for each level from grades three through eight. There are thirty-six lessons per manual, and each lesson is organized around a central theme or linguistic element.

Activities Each day, students explore one or more focus words through an activity, such as one of the following:

- Recognizing Context Clues
- Completing Sentences
- Identifying Related Words
- Finding Synonyms and Antonyms
- Using Exact Words
- Solving Analogies
- Unscrambling Letters
- Completing Word Webs, Chains, and Charts
- Matching Columns

Teacher's Notes For each daily activity, teacher notes provide the answer, define the focus word or words, and offer teaching tips or reinforcement activities. These activities allow students to apply their understanding of the focus word or words to a different context.

Extension Activity Included with each set of lessons is an optional extension activity, particularly suited to small-group work. This activity reviews the week's focus words, challenges students to brainstorm other words, or suggests projects that connect vocabulary building and specific content areas.

The Word List The focus words are a mix of grade-appropriate words and more challenging items—most are one or two grades beyond the students' level. The goal is to expand vocabulary as well as to review it. The focus words include those that students will find useful in their speaking, writing, and reading. Some of the words are important in subjects presented at a particular grade. Use the list of Themes and Focus Words to help you select lessons that support students' work in content areas across the curriculum.

How to Use *Daily Vocabulary*

Each day, write the activity on the board. Then choose the procedure that you prefer:

- Ask a student to give the answer orally. Write the answer on the board, and have students explain why it is or is not correct.
- Ask a student to come to the board and to write the answer to the activity. The student should then explain the answer.
- Ask students to copy the activity and then to write the answer in their journals. Next, have students offer their answers orally, and then write them on the board.

After students have completed the daily activity, ask them to record each focus word and its definition in their journals and to write a sentence that shows its meaning.

Time Management

Each day's activity requires about five to ten minutes. The lessons work best when the activities are presented daily rather than once a week for twenty-five minutes. Regular practice improves skill retention and impresses upon students that vocabulary building should be a daily, lifelong habit. If you wish, use the lessons to focus student attention during transition times such as the start of the school day or the period after recess or lunch.

Getting the Most from the Program

Daily Vocabulary is part of a complete language arts program, and it supports skills presented in *McDougal, Littell English* and *McDougal, Littell Spelling*. Regular, sustained use of *Daily Vocabulary* will strengthen your students' vocabulary skills and lay the groundwork for future success.

THEMES AND FOCUS WORDS

Week	Theme	Focus Words	Week	Theme	Focus Words
1	**Motion**	swoop, plunge and soar, hobble, amble, waddle	10	**Dinosaur Days**	prehistoric, fossil, extinct, habitat, vegetation
2	**Size**	miniature and puny, huge, gigantic and enormous, bulky, colossal and dwarfish	11	**Water**	evaporate, vapor, humidity, precipitation, condense
3	**Appearance**	transparent and sheer, dingy, grimy, sturdy, pale	12	**Simple Machines**	lever, pulley, axle, wedge, ramp
4	**Farms**	silo, sow and reap, bale, harvest, combine	13	**The Solar System**	planet, orbit, satellite, crater, meteor
5	**Pioneer Life**	prairie, wick, hearth, sod, buckboard	14	**The Prefix *re-***	rewrite, reappear, recount, rebound, rearrange
6	**Cities**	city, urban and rural, suburban, metropolitan, residential and commercial	15	**The Prefix *-un***	unlimited, unfortunate, unknown, unavailable, undisturbed
7	**Jobs**	messenger, engineer, physician, paramedic, optician	16	**The Prefix *dis-***	distrust, dissatisfied, dishonest, disobedient, disagree
8	**Newspapers**	headline, section, caption, reporter, editor	17	**The Suffixes *-er* and *-or***	photographer, landscaper, director and supervisor, employer, counselor
9	**Maps**	compass, scale, boundary, equator, hemisphere	18	**The Suffix *-less***	penniless, fearless, hopeless, worthless, heartless

Week	Theme	Focus Words	Week	Theme	Focus Words
19	The Suffix -*ful*	dreadful, plentiful, hurtful and merciful, mournful, eventful	28	Singing	chorus; duet, trio, and quartet; alto and soprano; tenor and bass; baritone
20	Measurement	mileage, circumference, meter and kilometer, square foot, acre	29	Theater	performance, rehearse, understudy, skit, dialogue
21	Solving Problems	multiply, product, graph, estimate, calculate	30	Computers	hardware, keyboard, screen, menu, command
22	Working with Numbers	dividend, divisor, quotient, average, fraction	31	More About Computers	data, program, disk, software, mouse
23	Folk Tales	enchant, transform, ogre, outwit, mysterious	32	Words from Names	braille, guppy, leotard, atlas, denim
24	Kinds of Stories	legend, myth, fable, fantasy, tall tale	33	Foods from Different Cultures	matzo, chowder, salsa, sushi, sauerkraut
25	Words for Reading	fiction and nonfiction, event, plot, character, setting	34	Sports	vault, dribble, punt, bunt, serve
26	Instruments from Different Cultures	sitar, marimba, maraca, gong, mandolin	35	Travel	passport, departure and arrival, tourist, brochure, schedule
27	Painting	mural and fresco, portrait, canvas, easel, palette	36	Radio and TV Jargon	sound bite, pan, laugh track, zoom, canned

DAY	FOCUS WORD	ACTIVITIES	TEACHER'S NOTES
1	**SWOOP**	Choose the best word to complete the sentence. The sea gull _____ into the sea to catch a fish. **a.** goes **b.** swoops **c.** stumbles **d.** trots	**Answer:** *b. swoops* The focus word *swoop* means "to rush down or pounce suddenly" and suggests speed and power. Unlike the word *go*, the word *swoop* describes a specific type of movement. The word *stumble* means "to miss a step," and the word *trot* means "to move quickly" and suggests the gait of a horse.
2	**PLUNGE** **SOAR**	Which word does not belong with the others? swoop, dive, plunge, soar	**Answer:** *soar* The focus words *plunge* and *soar* have opposite meanings. *Plunge* means "to leap or dive suddenly." *Soar* means "to rise in the air." **Reinforcement Activity:** Have students complete this analogy. *Diver* is to *plunge* as _____ is to *soar*. **Possible Answers:** *bird, basketball player, airplane*
3	**HOBBLE**	Give a synonym for the word *hobbled* in the following sentence. After twisting my ankle, I hobbled around for weeks.	**Possible Answer:** *limped* The phrase "after twisting my ankle" provides a context clue for *hobble*, which means "to walk with difficulty." You may wish to have students mention some accidents that might cause a person to hobble, such as stubbing a toe, stepping on a tack, or tripping on a stair.

DAY	FOCUS WORD	ACTIVITIES	TEACHER'S NOTES
4	AMBLE	Which word would be a good substitute for *walked* in the following sentence? We walked along the shore and gazed at the moon. **a.** hobbled **b.** dashed **c.** galloped **d.** ambled	**Answer:** *d. ambled* *Amble* means "to walk at a slow, easy pace." The words *galloped* and *dashed* suggest too much haste for gazing at the moon. You may wish to have students list two or more antonyms for *amble*, such as *rush, hurry, speed,* or *run*.
5	WADDLE	Solve the following analogy: *Duck* is to *waddle* as *snake* is to _____. duck : waddle :: snake : _____	**Possible Answer:** *slither* *Waddle* means "to walk with short steps, swaying from side to side like a duck." You might have students list other animals and describe their characteristic movements. For example, a peacock struts, and a squirrel scurries.

OPTIONAL EXTENSION ACTIVITY

This can be an individual or small-group activity. Have students list as many words as they can that describe movement. Then have them arrange the words in order from the slowest to the fastest movement.

Possible Answers: *limp, walk, skip, race, fly, zoom*

Daily Vocabulary   Level 3

DAY	FOCUS WORD	ACTIVITIES	TEACHER'S NOTES
1	MINIATURE PUNY	Would you rather have a poodle that is miniature or puny? Explain why.	**Possible Answer:** *miniature* The word *miniature* means "on a small scale," but it doesn't mean "weak in size or power" as does the word *puny.* You might have students decide which of the two words work better in the following sentence: The coach said the player was too _____ to play football. **Answer:** *puny*
2	HUGE	Solve the following analogy: *Elephant* is to *huge* as *mouse* is to _____. elephant : huge :: mouse : _____	**Possible Answers:** *tiny, small* The word *huge* means "very large." Have students suggest other pairs of animals for the analogy, such as giraffe and sparrow, whale and minnow, and walrus and ant.
3	GIGANTIC ENORMOUS	Which word is not a synonym for *large* in the following sentence? Some dinosaurs were large creatures. **a.** huge **b.** gigantic **c.** enormous **d.** miniature	**Answer:** *d. miniature* Make sure that students understand that the focus words *gigantic* and *enormous* are synonyms. *Gigantic* means "like a giant" (as in size, weight, or strength). *Enormous* means "unusually large." You might ask students which word sounds bigger and have them name some things to which these words might apply, such as mountains, castles, skyscrapers, and gorillas.

DAY	FOCUS WORD	ACTIVITIES	TEACHER'S NOTES
4	**BULKY**	Name two or more synonyms for *bulky* in the following sentence: The carton was too bulky to fit through the doorway.	**Possible Answers:** *large, big, sizable, immense* *Bulky* means "large and awkward to handle" but does not imply heaviness. Something light in weight can still be bulky. Ask students to provide examples, such as a box containing pillows or lampshades.
5	**COLOSSAL** **DWARFISH**	Add words to the word map. 	**Possible Answers:** opposite meaning—*little, tiny, miniature, puny, small*, . . . ; similar meaning—*large, huge, gigantic, immense*, . . . The final focus words for this week are antonyms. *Colossal* means "very large," and *dwarfish* means "much smaller than normal." The word *colossal* comes from the word *Colossus*, the name of a gigantic statue of Apollo at the entrance to the harbor of the Greek island of Rhodes.

OPTIONAL EXTENSION ACTIVITY

Divide the class into several small groups and have each group brainstorm additional words that describe size. When each group has compiled a list of several words, have a member of one group call out a word. Ask a member of another group to create a sentence using the word and to write it on the board. For example, for the word *towering,* a possible sentence might be the following: An eagle perched on the towering peak of a mountain.

Daily Vocabulary — Level 3

DAY	FOCUS WORD	ACTIVITIES	TEACHER'S NOTES
1	**TRANSPARENT** **SHEER**	Choose the correct answer: If a piece of plastic is transparent, it **a.** cannot be cut **b.** is enormous **c.** can be seen through **d.** will shatter if dropped	**Answer:** *c. can be seen through* The focus words are synonyms. *Transparent* means "clear enough or thin enough to be seen through." *Sheer*, which means "very thin or transparent," is often applied to fabrics, such as nylon or silk. **Reinforcement Activity:** Have students give a synonym for these words. **Possible Answers:** *clear, glassy, thin, gauzy*
2	**DINGY**	Give two or more synonyms for *dingy* in the following sentence. The princess lived not in a shining palace but in a dingy cellar.	**Possible Answers:** *dark, dismal, grimy, gloomy, murky* The opposite phrase "shining palace" provides a context clue for *dingy*, which means "rather dark and dirty." You might have students create analogies for the word *dingy*; for example, dingy : dark :: bright : shining.
3	**GRIMY**	What word would best describe a toddler's hands if he or she had just made mud pies? **a.** bruised **b.** spotless **c.** clean **d.** grimy	**Answer:** *d. grimy* The focus word *grimy* means "full of dirt." Students might list other words to describe grimy hands, such as *dirty, soiled, muddy, messy, grubby,* and *filthy*.

Daily Vocabulary   *Level* 3

DAY	FOCUS WORD	ACTIVITIES	TEACHER'S NOTES
4	STURDY	Choose the correct answer. A sturdy house **a.** glows in the dark **b.** is made of straw **c.** looks grimy **d.** is solidly built	**Answer:** *d. is solidly built* The word *sturdy* means "strongly built or constructed." **Reinforcement Activity:** Have students complete the following analogy: *Sturdy* is to *weak* as *sunny* is to _____. **Possible Answers:** *gloomy, dark*
5	PALE	Which word does not belong with the others? pale, colorless, light, gloomy	**Answer:** *gloomy*; it does not describe something light in color. *Pale* means "of a whitish or colorless complexion." You might present other synonyms for *pale*, such as *wan* or *ashen*, using a crossword.

Crossword:
```
        P
    W A N
        L
  A S H E N
```

OPTIONAL EXTENSION ACTIVITY

Some words that describe appearance have positive meanings; others do not. Have students list words that describe an attractive appearance. Then have them list words that describe an unattractive appearance. Encourage them to include some of this week's vocabulary words as well as other descriptive words that they know.

Possible Answers:

Attractive	Unattractive
sheer	dingy
fresh	grimy
bright	dull
beautiful	run-down

Daily Vocabulary

Level 3

DAY	FOCUS WORD	ACTIVITIES	TEACHER'S NOTES
1	SILO	What would you not expect to find on a farm? **a.** a tractor **b.** a barn **c.** a silo **d.** a vending machine	**Answer:** *d. a vending machine* The focus word *silo* means "a building on a farm where food for livestock is stored." **Reinforcement Activity:** Students might draw a picture of a farmhouse, a silo, and a barn.
2	SOW REAP	What do the words *sow* and *reap* mean in the following sentence? In the spring, farmers sow seeds; in the fall, they reap crops.	**Answer:** *Sow* means "to plant or scatter (as seed) for growing"; *reap* means "to harvest by cutting." Make sure that students recognize that these words have opposite meanings. **Reinforcement Activity:** Have students complete this analogy: *Sow* is to *reap* as *begin* is to _____. **Possible Answers:** *end, finish, complete*
3	BALE	How do the homonyms *bale* and *bail* differ in meaning? Bales of hay were scattered across the field. We had to bail several inches of water from our canoe.	**Answer:** The focus word *bale* means "a large bundle of goods tightly tied for storing or shipping." *Bail* means "to dip and throw out water from a boat." **Reinforcement Activity:** Have students try this analogy: *Bale* is to *hay* as *carton* is to _____. **Possible Answers:** *eggs, milk, juice*

DAY	FOCUS WORD	ACTIVITIES	TEACHER'S NOTES
4	**HARVEST**	Give a synonym for the word *harvest* in the following sentence. The farmer wants to harvest the wheat before the first frost.	**Possible Answers:** *gather, collect, reap,* or *cut* *Harvest* means "to gather in a crop." As a noun, it means "the season when crops are gathered." For reinforcement, have students suggest antonyms for *harvest*, such as *sow* or *plant.*
5	**COMBINE**	Choose the best word to complete the sentence. Sarah drove a _____ during August to reap the wheat more quickly. **a.** silo **b.** bus **c.** combine **d.** elevator	**Answer:** *c. combine* The word *combine* means a "machine that harvests grain." To help students associate this word with the words *reap* and *crop*, you might give them a simple crossword.

OPTIONAL EXTENSION ACTIVITY

Ask students what farmers do, what tools they use, and what buildings can be found on a farm. You may wish to list their answers on the board in columns.

Possible Answers:

Activities	Tools	Buildings
sow	combine	silo
reap	tractor	barn
fertilize	plow	farmhouse

DAY	FOCUS WORD	ACTIVITIES	TEACHER'S NOTES
1	**PRAIRIE**	Choose the best word to complete the sentence. Herds of buffalo once roamed the _____. **a.** cliffs **b.** prairie **c.** shore **d.** forest	**Answer:** *b. prairie* The focus word *prairie* means "a large area of level or rolling grassland." **Reinforcement Activity:** Have students complete the following analogy. *Prairie* is to *grass* as *forest* is to _____. **Possible Answer:** *trees*
2	**WICK**	Add one or more related words to the following list: flame, wick, candle	**Possible Answers:** *wax, lantern* All the words relate to making light. *Wick* means "a cord or a bundle of threads that burns in a small, steady flame." **Reinforcement Activity:** Using a chart, contrast pioneer life and modern life. <table><tr><td>**Pioneer Life**</td><td>**Modern Life**</td></tr><tr><td>wicks and candles</td><td>electric lights</td></tr></table>
3	**HEARTH**	What would you not expect to find in a pioneer house on a prairie? **a.** lantern **b.** hearth **c.** skillet **d.** electric toaster	**Answer:** *d. electric toaster* *Hearth* means "an area, often made of brick or stone, in front of a fireplace." You may have to point out that *skillet* means "a large frying pan." **Reinforcement Activity:** Ask students why a pioneer would not make a hearth out of paper, wood, or cardboard. **Possible Answer:** These materials could easily catch fire.

DAY	FOCUS WORD	ACTIVITIES	TEACHER'S NOTES
4	**SOD**	What do you think the word *sod* means in the following sentence? Many pioneers on the plains built houses out of dirt and sod.	**Possible Answer:** blocks of grass The focus word *sod* means "the layer of the soil filled with roots." You might draw on the board a simple crossword to reinforce the meaning of this word. S E E D S O D I R T
5	**BUCKBOARD**	Which word does not belong with the others? buckboard barge wagon carriage stagecoach	**Answer:** *barge*; it is a water craft The focus word *buckboard* means "a four-wheeled carriage with a seat that rests on a springy platform." **Reinforcement Activity:** Have students complete the following analogy. *Buckboard* is to *past* as *autombile* is to _____. **Answer:** *present*

OPTIONAL EXTENSION ACTIVITY

Ask students to explain how pioneers might have used the following items. Students should consult dictionaries to find the meanings of any terms that they do not know.

Item	Use
churn	to make butter
ax	to chop wood
calico cloth	to make clothes
buckboard	to take short trips

Daily Vocabulary   Level 3

DAY	FOCUS WORD	ACTIVITIES	TEACHER'S NOTES
1	CITY	Arrange the following names of places from smallest to largest: country state county city town continent	**Answer:** town, city, county, state, country, continent The focus word *city* means "a place in which people live that is larger than a town." You might ask students to name cities they would like to visit or to live in when they grow up and to explain why.
2	URBAN RURAL	Solve the following analogy: *Sidewalks* are to *urban* as _____ are to *rural*. sidewalks : urban :: _____ : rural	**Possible Answers:** *paths, trails* *Urban* means "of or relating to a city." *Rural* means "of or relating to the country." **Reinforcement Activity:** Using a chart, contrast urban and rural areas. | Urban	Rural
---	---
shopping malls taxicabs	farms tractors	
3	SUBURBAN	What would you probably not find in a suburban area? **a.** a library **b.** a motel **c.** a silo **d.** a train station	**Answer:** *c. a silo;* it is found on a farm *Suburban* means "of or relating to the area just outside a city," so a silo would probably not be found in that kind of area. **Reinforcement Activity:** Have students name other things found in a suburban area.

DAY	FOCUS WORD	ACTIVITIES	TEACHER'S NOTES
4	METROPOLITAN	Choose the correct ending to complete the sentence. If you were given a tour of the New York City metropolitan area, you would probably see **a.** tractors **b.** fields **c.** museums, theaters, and skyscrapers **d.** dirt roads	**Answer:** *c. museums, theaters, and skyscrapers* The focus word *metropolitan* means "of or relating to a large city and smaller surrounding communities." **Reinforcement Activity:** Have students name and describe some metropolitan areas that they have visited or read about.
5	RESIDENTIAL COMMERCIAL	Add one or more examples to each column in the chart below. CITY Residential Areas — houses Commercial Areas — businesses	**Possible Answers:** *Residential*—apartments, children, lawns, schools, parks; *Commercial*—restaurants, clothing stores, supermarkets, record stores The focus words refer to urban areas where people live or do business. *Residential* means "suitable for or containing homes"; *commercial* means "having to do with business."

OPTIONAL EXTENSION ACTIVITY

Have students make a map of an imaginary metropolitan area. Ask them to label the urban and suburban areas. They should also label residential and commercial areas and several things that might be found in these areas, such as important streets, parks, museums,

DAY	FOCUS WORD	ACTIVITIES	TEACHER'S NOTES
1	**MESSENGER**	Choose the best word to complete the sentence. The _____ delivered a telegram to my grandmother. **a.** painter **b.** writer **c.** messenger **d.** clerk	**Answer:** *c. messenger* The phrase "delivered a telegram" provides a context clue for *messenger*, which means "a person who carries a message or goes on an errand." You may wish to have students give examples of other workers who make deliveries, such as mail carriers, newspaper carriers, and truck drivers.
2	**ENGINEER**	What different meanings does the word *engineer* have in these two sentences? The engineer stopped the train when he saw a cow standing on the tracks. A well-known engineer helped design the new post office on State Street.	**Answer:** *Engineer* in the first sentence refers to a person who operates a train. *Engineer* in the second sentence refers to a person who designs heating systems, plumbing systems, and other systems for a building. Explain that design engineers also create plans for such things as cars, roads, bridges, and computers. **Reinforcement Activity:** Invite students to name things they would like to design if they were engineers.
3	**PHYSICIAN**	Which word does not belong with the others? Tell why it does not belong. dentist, farmer, physician, nurse	**Answer:** *farmer*; it does not name a health care worker *Physician* means "a specialist in healing human disease." You might have students give a synonym for *physician*. (**Answer:** *doctor*) **Reinforcement Activity:** Have students complete the following analogy. *Physician* is to *hospital* as _____ is to *store*. **Possible Answers:** *clerk, salesperson, cashier*

DAY	FOCUS WORD	ACTIVITIES	TEACHER'S NOTES
4	PARAMEDIC	How do physicians and paramedics differ?	**Answer:** Physicians prescribe medicine and have more training than do paramedics, who usually provide only a few emergency services. **Reinforcement Activity:** Have students give examples of situations in which paramedics are needed, such as car accidents, airplane crashes, and accidents in the home.

5	OPTICIAN	Complete the following analogy:
		
		   Dentist is to *teeth* as *optician* is to _____.
		
		   dentist : teeth :: optician : _____
			Answer: *eyes*
			
			An optician makes eyeglasses and contact lenses. Challenge students to identify the profession of a person who checks the eyes and prescribes eyeglasses or contact lenses to correct vision problems.
			
			Answer: *optometrist.*

OPTIONAL EXTENSION ACTIVITY

Have students brainstorm a list of job titles. Write their suggestions on the board. Then have them take turns creating riddles for each job, perhaps in this form:

   I drive people where they want to go. I know most streets in this city. Who am I?

Answer: *a taxicab driver*

DAY	FOCUS WORD	ACTIVITIES	TEACHER'S NOTES
1	**HEADLINE**	Choose the best answer to the following question. Where would you find a headline? **a.** in the attic **b.** on top of your head **c.** in a bottle cap **d.** in a newspaper	**Answer:** *d. in a newspaper* The focus word *headline* means "a title that appears with a newspaper article." **Reinforcement Activity:** Using a newspaper, point out some headlines to students. Then ask them what else they notice about headlines. **Possible Answers:** They are short. They are informative. The words are big in size.
2	**SECTION**	Complete the following analogy. *Section* is to *newspaper* as *chapter* is to _____. section : newspaper :: chapter : _____	**Answer:** *book* A section is a main part of a newspaper. It contains information on one topic, such as sports or business. A chapter is a main part of a book. **Reinforcement Activity:** Using a newspaper you have brought to class, have students point out and identify each main section.
3	**CAPTION**	Choose the correct answer for the following question. Which item always appears above a caption? **a.** an advertisement **b.** an article **c.** a picture **d.** a title	**Answer:** *c. a picture* The focus word *caption* means "a comment or title that appears below a picture." **Reinforcement Activity:** Cut pictures out of newspapers. Have students create captions for those pictures.

DAY	FOCUS WORD	ACTIVITIES	TEACHER'S NOTES
4	REPORTER	Add related words to the word web. *[word web diagram: activities — REPORTER — tools]*	**Possible Answers:** activities—*interviews, writes;* tools—*note pad, pencil, microphone* The focus word *reporter* means "a person who gathers facts and writes reports for a newspaper or magazine." **Reinforcement Activity:** Ask students to tell where they have seen or heard reporters **Possible Answers:** on television, on the street, on the radio
5	EDITOR	Mr. White is the editor of *The Daily Planet* newspaper. What do these paragraphs suggest about his job? Mr. White told Jimmy Olsen to write a report about Superman. The next day, Mr. White said, "Great job, Jim! Your article will appear in tomorrow's paper."	**Possible Answer:** Mr. White decides what articles will appear in his newspaper. The focus word *editor* means "a person who is the head of a department of a newspaper or magazine." **Reinforcement Activity:** Ask students what questions they would ask a newspaper editor about his or her work.

OPTIONAL EXTENSION ACTIVITY

Ask students to write a newspaper headline for a recent event in your classroom or school. Point out to students that headlines are usually short and should grab the reader's attention. You might wish to remind students that they should capitalize the first, last, and every other important word in their titles.

Possible Answers: *Third Graders Have Bake Sale, Student Wins Award, Computers Go to School*

Daily Vocabulary
Level 3

DAY	FOCUS WORD	ACTIVITIES	TEACHER'S NOTES
1	COMPASS	Complete the following analogy. *Compass* is to *direction* as *watch* is to _____. compass : direction :: watch : _____	**Answer:** *time* The focus word *compass* means "an instrument used for showing direction, consisting of a magnetic needle that points toward the north." You might show students a compass and explain how it works. Help students to recognize north, south, east, and west.
2	SCALE	Why might you use the scale on a map?	**Answer:** to learn the number of miles between places *Scale* means "a series of spaces marked off by lines and used for measuring distances." Draw this scale on the board. 0 100 200 If one inch stands for 100 miles, ask students how many miles separate two cities that are four inches apart. (**Answer:** 400 miles)
3	BOUNDARY	Cross out the word that does not belong with the others. Tell why it does not belong. boundary, border, area, edge	**Answer:** *area;* it is not a dividing line The focus word *boundary* means "any line or thing marking a limit or border." **Reinforcement Activity:** Have students point out the state boundaries on a map of the United States. Then ask them to identify other boundaries on the map, such as the boundaries dividing land and bodies of water.

DAY	FOCUS WORD	ACTIVITIES	TEACHER'S NOTES
4	EQUATOR	What would you not expect to find at the equator? **a.** land **b.** snow **c.** water **d.** hot weather	**Answer:** *b. snow* The focus word *equator* means "an imaginary circle around the earth that divides the earth's surface into the Northern and Southern Hemispheres." All areas around the equator are warm. **Reinforcement Activity:** Ask a student to point out the equator on a world map or globe. Then ask students to identify the countries at or near the equator.
5	HEMISPHERE	If *hemi-* means "half" and *sphere* means "a globe or ball," what does *hemisphere* mean?	**Possible Answers:** *half of a ball; half of a globe; half of the earth* The focus word *hemisphere* means "any of the halves of the earth." **Reinforcement Activity:** Using a globe, have a student point out the northern and southern hemispheres.

OPTIONAL EXTENSION ACTIVITY

Write the word *MAP* on the board and have students name as many related words as possible. List these words on the board. Then work with the students to help them sort the words into categories and arrange the categories around *MAP* to form a web.

Possible Answers: countries—*United States, Brazil, England;* cities—*San Juan, Chicago, Boston;* land formations—*forests, mountains, canyons;* bodies of water—*oceans, lakes, rivers*

DAY	FOCUS WORD	ACTIVITIES	TEACHER'S NOTES

1	**PREHISTORIC**	Choose the best word to complete the sentence.
		
		The dinosaurs lived in _____ times.
		
		    a. frontier
		    b. modern
		    c. prehistoric
		    d. recent
			Answer: *c. prehistoric*
			
			Prehistoric means "living before written history began." Explain that this word is formed by adding the prefix *pre-*, which means "before," to the word *historic*, which means "written records of the past."
			
			Reinforcement Activity: Have students name other words containing the prefix *pre-*.
			
			Possible Answers: *prepay, precook, preview.*

2	**FOSSIL**	Make a word chain. In each blank, write a word that connects to the word that comes before or after it. _____ ➡ *fossil* ➡ *reptile* ➡ _____ ➡ _____	**Possible Answers:** *dinosaur, (fossil), (reptile), turtle, shell* The focus word *fossil* means "the remains of a plant or animal from the past." **Reinforcement Activity:** Have students complete this analogy: *Fossil* is to *prehistoric* as *computer* is to _____. **Answer:** *modern*
3	**EXTINCT**	Complete the following analogy: *Hot* is to *cold* as *extinct* is to _____. hot : cold :: extinct : _____	**Possible Answer:** *living* *Extinct*, which means "no longer in existence or use," describes things that have died off. **Reinforcement Activity:** Ask students to name something that is extinct. Then ask them to suggest the word that refers to plants and animals in danger of dying off. **Answers:** *dinosaurs, endangered*

DAY	FOCUS WORD	ACTIVITIES	TEACHER'S NOTES
4	HABITAT	Match each animal on the left to its natural habitat on the right. shark jungle dinosaur ocean tiger plain	**Answers:** *shark—ocean; dinosaur—plain; tiger—jungle* The focus word *habitat* means "the region where a plant or animal naturally grows or lives." **Reinforcement Activity:** Ask students to give other examples of plants and animals and their habitats. **Possible Answers:** *deer, fox—woods; trout, salmon—lake, ocean; cactus—desert*
5	VEGETATION	Name some forms of vegetation that existed at the time of the dinosaurs.	**Possible Answers:** *grass, trees, bushes, ferns* The focus word *vegetation* means "plant life." Point out to students that some dinosaurs were plant-eaters while others were meat-eaters. **Reinforcement Activity:** Have students unscramble the letters *l t p s n a* to make a word that is a synonym for vegetation. **Answer:** *plants*

OPTIONAL EXTENSION ACTIVITY

Invite students to work in pairs to create labeled drawings or dioramas of the world of the dinosaurs. Encourage students to consult encyclopedias and other reference materials.

Daily Vocabulary

Level 3

DAY	FOCUS WORD	ACTIVITIES	TEACHER'S NOTES
1	EVAPORATE	Choose the word or phrase that best completes the sentence. If you boil water in a pan, some of the water will _____, or escape into the air. **a.** melt **b.** form ice cubes **c.** evaporate **d.** turn different colors	**Answer:** *c. evaporate* The focus word *evaporate* means "to escape into the air in the form of a gas." Explain to students that water is made up of tiny invisible particles called molecules. These molecules are always moving. As they move, some escape into the air. **Reinforcement Activity:** Ask students why they think heat makes water evaporate faster. **Answer:** Heat makes the molecules move faster.
2	VAPOR	Circle the smaller word inside *evaporate*. What do you think it means? evaporate	**Answer:** *vapor;* a gas formed as water evaporates The focus word *vapor* means "water in the form of a gas." Vapor is formed during the process of evaporation. **Reinforcement Activity:** Ask students how they could create vapor. **Possible Answer:** by heating a pan of water
3	HUMIDITY	Which word does not belong with the others? Tell why it does not belong. humidity dampness dryness moisture	**Answer:** *dryness;* it does not suggest wetness. The focus word *humidity* means "the amount of moisture in the air." **Reinforcement Activity:** Have students discuss why people feel uncomfortable on a warm day with high humidity. **Possible Answer:** The large amount of moisture in the air does not allow the perspiration on the skin to evaporate.

DAY	FOCUS WORD	ACTIVITIES	TEACHER'S NOTES
4	PRECIPITATION	Complete the following analogy: *Rain* is to *precipitation* as *shirt* is to _____. rain : precipitation :: shirt : _____	**Possible Answer:** *clothing* Rain is a type of precipitation, which means "water that falls to the earth as rain, sleet, snow, mist, or hail." A shirt is a type of clothing. **Reinforcement Activity:** Ask what problems are caused by too much or too little precipitation. **Possible Answers:** flooding, drought, crop loss
5	CONDENSE	Choose the best word to complete the following sentence. When water vapor _____, it changes from a gas into a liquid. a. evaporates b. condenses c. disappears d. expands	**Answer:** *b. condenses* The focus word *condense* means "to change from a gas into a liquid." **Reinforcement Activity:** Remind students that heat makes water evaporate. Ask them if the air must get warmer or cooler in order for water vapor to become liquid water again. **Possible Answer:** The air must get cooler.

OPTIONAL EXTENSION ACTIVITY

Draw the diagram on the board. Ask students to use as many new words as possible to describe what is going on in the diagram.

Possible Answer: 1. Water *evaporates* and becomes *vapor*. 2. Vapor *condenses* and forms a cloud. 3. The cloud cools and creates *precipitation*.

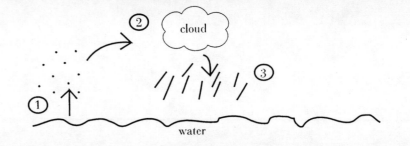

DAY	FOCUS WORD	ACTIVITIES	TEACHER'S NOTES
1	**LEVER**	Choose the best word to complete the following sentence. Use a lever when you want to _____ a heavy object. **a.** crush **b.** build **c.** bend **d.** lift	**Answer:** *d. lift* The focus word *lever* means "a stiff bar for lifting a weight." You may wish to draw a picture of a lever on the board to reinforce the meaning of this word. weight → ◻ △ ← support, ← lever
2	**PULLEY**	If you had a pulley, what might you use it for?	**Possible Answers:** raising a sign, lifting furniture, pulling something out of a hole *Pulley* means "a wheel on which a belt, rope, or chain runs." A pulley raises a weight attached at one end when someone pulls on the other end. pulley, ← belt, rope, or chain, ← weight
3	**AXLE**	Which word does not belong with the others? Tell why it does not belong. axle pulley windshield lever	**Answer:** *windshield;* it is not the name of a simple machine. The focus word *axle* means "a rod on which a wheel or a pair of wheels turns." **Reinforcement Activity:** Ask students to name things that have axles. **Possible Answers:** *cars, trucks*

DAY	FOCUS WORD	ACTIVITIES	TEACHER'S NOTES
4	WEDGE	Match the best machine to the job. raising a flag lever lifting a crate wedge making a hole pulley splitting wood drill	**Possible Answers:** *raising a flag—pulley, lifting a crate—lever, making a hole— drill, splitting wood— wedge* The focus word *wedge* means "a piece of wood or metal that tapers to a thin edge and is used for splitting something or for raising something heavy."
5	RAMP	Where do you see ramps in and around your school?	**Possible Answers:** beside stairways, leading up to doors The focus word *ramp* means "a sloping platform or roadway connecting different levels." **Reinforcement Activity:** Ask students to explain why ramps are used. **Possible Answer:** to slide or roll objects from one level to another

OPTIONAL EXTENSION ACTIVITY

Invite students to work in pairs or small teams to create simple machines, using toys and classroom materials, such as rubber bands, cellophane tape, paper clips, popsicle sticks, cardboard, straws, and pencils. Allow students to demonstrate how their machines work.

Daily Vocabulary   *Level 3*

DAY	FOCUS WORD	ACTIVITIES	TEACHER'S NOTES
1	**PLANET**	Our solar system contains nine planets. Name as many of them as you can.	**Answer:** Mercury, Venus, Earth, Mars, Jupiter, Saturn, Uranus, Neptune, and Pluto The focus word *planet* means "a large body that travels around the sun." **Reinforcement Activity:** The word *planet* comes from a Greek word meaning "wanderer." Ask students how the planets are like wanderers. **Possible Answer:** The planets are always moving, traveling around the sun.

2	**ORBIT**	Which word would be a good substitute for *go around* in the following sentence?
		
		   It takes the earth about 365 days to go around the sun.
		
		   a. eclipse
		   b. orbit
		   c. escape
		   d. reflect
			Answer: *b. orbit*
			
			The focus word *orbit*, which means "to move in a circular path," is often used to describe the movement of planets around the sun.
			
			Reinforcement Activity: Have students name the planet that takes the shortest time to orbit the sun.
			
			Answer: Mercury, the planet closest to the sun, takes the shortest time.

3	**SATELLITE**	Complete the analogy.
		
		   Satellite is to *planet* as *earth* is to _____.
		
		   satellite : planet :: earth : _____
			Answer: *sun*
			
			The focus word *satellite* means "a smaller body that revolves around a planet," much like the earth revolves around the sun. A satellite can be either natural or artificial. Our moon is a natural satellite of the earth. Several artificial satellites also orbit the earth, performing many tasks, such as photographing cloud formations or transmitting television signals.

DAY	FOCUS WORD	ACTIVITIES	TEACHER'S NOTES
4	CRATER	Which word does not belong with the others? crater pit hill ditch hole	**Answer:** *hill;* it is not a type of hole The focus word *crater* means "a hole (as in the surface of the earth or the moon) formed by an impact (as of a meteorite)." **Reinforcement Activity:** Have students complete the following analogy: *Crater* is to *deep* as *mountain* is to _____. **Possible Answer:** *high*
5	METEOR	Choose the best word to complete the sentence. Sometimes a shooting star, or _____, flashes across the night sky. **a.** planet **b.** meteor **c.** satellite **d.** crater	**Answer:** *b. meteor* The phrase "a shooting star" provides a context clue for *meteor*, which means "a small piece of matter that produces a fiery streak as it passes through the earth's atmosphere."

OPTIONAL EXTENSION ACTIVITY

Challenge students to search for pictures that illustrate the words presented in this week's lesson. Encourage them to check science books and books about space travel, to photocopy and label the pictures, and to mount them on poster board for display in the classroom. As an alternative, students might make models of the solar system, labeling each of the nine planets.

DAY	FOCUS WORD	ACTIVITIES	TEACHER'S NOTES
1	**REWRITE**	Choose the correct answer to complete the sentence. _____ + *write* means "to make a piece of writing better." **a.** un- **b.** re- **c.** pre- **d.** inter-	**Answer:** *b.* re- *Rewrite* means "to write again in different words or a different form." The prefix *re-* means "again" or "back." The spelling of the base word does not change when *re-* is added to it. **Reinforcement Activity:** Have students name people who do much writing and rewriting in their daily work, such as lawyers, reporters, editors, novelists, and poets.
2	**REAPPEAR**	Add *re-* to one of the words to make the following sentence clearer. Robins go away in the fall but appear each spring.	**Answer:** *Re-* should be added to *appear.* The word *reappear* means "to appear again" and describes the return of robins each spring. You may wish to have students mention other things that reappear each spring, such as buds, flowers, leaves, children in the park, and baseball teams.
3	**RECOUNT**	What two meanings does the word *recount* have in the following sentences? She recounted to me some of her adventures as a mountain climber. After a close election, a candidate may ask to have the votes recounted.	**Answer:** In the first sentence, the focus word *recount* means "to tell in detail"; in the second sentence, *recount* means "to count again." Make sure that students understand that they should examine the context of a word for clues to its meaning.

DAY	FOCUS WORD	ACTIVITIES	TEACHER'S NOTES
4	REBOUND	Choose the best word to complete the sentence. The basketball player leaped for the ball as it _____ from the backboard. **a.** reappeared **b.** recounted **c.** rebounded **d.** hobbled	**Answer:** *c. rebounded* The focus word *rebound* means "to spring back after hitting something." **Reinforcement Activity:** Have students indicate which of the following objects can rebound: a hockey puck, a wristwatch, a soccer ball, a notebook, a jump-rope, a wallet, a beachball. **Answer:** *a hockey puck, a soccer ball, and a beachball*
5	REARRANGE	Choose the correct answer. If you rearrange the books on your desk, you **a.** put new covers on them **b.** read each one again **c.** throw out the old ones **d.** change their positions	**Answer:** *d. change their positions* The focus word *rearrange* means "to arrange again, usually in a different way." Ask students to name several things they might rearrange, such as flowers, toys, tools, dishes, and furniture.

OPTIONAL EXTENSION ACTIVITY

Invite students to use the prefix *re-* to write a word with the same meaning as each pair of words below.

tie again (retie)	read again (reread)
do again (redo)	teach again (reteach)
check again (recheck)	visit again (revisit)
fill again (refill)	paint again (repaint)
use again (reuse)	view again (review)

DAY	FOCUS WORD	ACTIVITIES	TEACHER'S NOTES
1	**UNLIMITED**	Choose the correct answer to complete the sentence. _____ *limited* means "having no limits or controls." **a.** un- **b.** dis- **c.** pre- **d.** re-	**Answer:** *a. un-* The focus word *unlimited* is formed by adding the prefix *un-*, which means "not" or "opposite of," to the base word *limited*. Make sure that students recognize that adding the prefix *un-* does not change the spelling of a base word.
2	**UNFORTUNATE**	Add *un-* to one of the words so that the following sentence will make sense. My fortunate accident led to my missing the championship game.	**Answer:** *Un-* should be added to *fortunate*. The focus word *unfortunate* means "not fortunate; unlucky." **Reinforcement Activity:** Have students give one or more antonyms of *unfortunate*. **Possible Answers:** *lucky, successful*
3	**UNKNOWN**	Solve the following analogy: *Unknown* is to _____ as *wet* is to *dry*. unknown : _____ : : wet : dry	**Possible Answer:** *famous* The focus word unknown means "not known." **Reinforcement Activity:** Have students list other antonyms of *unknown*, such as *well-known, noted, familiar,* or *popular*.

Daily Vocabulary　　Level 3

DAY	FOCUS WORD	ACTIVITIES	TEACHER'S NOTES
4	UNAVAILABLE	Choose the correct answer. A doctor who is unavailable **a.** treats only infants and children **b.** works only in a hospital **c.** cannot see you right now **d.** is unknown in the community	**Answer:** *c. cannot see you right now* The focus word *unavailable* means "not available; impossible to get." **Reinforcement Activity:** Have students suggest reasons why a doctor might be *unavailable* on a particular day. **Possible Answers:** He or she might be ill, have gone out of town, or been called away on an emergency.
5	UNDISTURBED	Have students add synonyms to the word web. calm — UNDISTURBED	**Possible Answers:** *cool, peaceful, steady* **Reinforcement Activity:** Have students complete this analogy. *Undisturbed* is to _____ as *pleased* is to *angry*. **Possible Answers:** *upset, nervous, troubled*

OPTIONAL EXTENSION ACTIVITY

Have students work in teams of three to brainstorm a list of ten words that contain the prefix *un-*. After generating this list, students should write each word on a separate card. A member of an opposing team should then draw a card and try to determine the meaning of the word it contains. A correct answer is worth ten points. If a player answers incorrectly, the other team gets a chance to select a card. The team with the highest score wins.

Daily Vocabulary   Level 3

DAY	FOCUS WORD	ACTIVITIES	TEACHER'S NOTES
1	**DISTRUST**	Choose the correct answer to complete the sentence. _____ + *trust* means "not to trust." **a.** un- **b.** dis- **c.** re- **d.** pre-	**Answer:** *b. dis-* *Distrust* means "to have no trust or confidence in." The word is formed by adding the prefix *dis-*, which means "not" or "the opposite of," to the base word *trust*. **Reinforcement Activity:** Ask students to give reasons why they might distrust someone. **Possible Answers:** for telling lies, picking on somebody, getting others in trouble, or stealing things
2	**DISSATISFIED**	Add *dis-* to a word so that the following sentence will make sense. I was satisfied with my low grade in spelling.	**Answer:** *Dis-* should be added to *satisfied*. The phrase "my low grade in spelling" provides a context clue to the meaning of *dissatisfied*, which means "not satisfied; not pleased." **Reinforcement Activity:** Have students give one or more antonyms for *dissatisfied*. **Possible Answers:** *satisfied, pleased, content*
3	**DISHONEST**	Add related words to the word web. false — DISHONEST	**Possible Answers:** *two-faced, untrue, tricky* The focus word *dishonest* means "not honest or trustworthy." **Reinforcement Activity:** Have students complete the following analogy: *Dishonest* is to *crooked* as *honest* is to _____. **Possible Answers:** *truthful, honorable, trustworthy*

DAY	FOCUS WORD	ACTIVITIES	TEACHER'S NOTES
4	**DISOBEDIENT**	Choose the best phrase to complete the sentence. A disobedient pet is likely to _____. **a.** come when called **b.** greet you at the door **c.** learn new tricks **d.** ignore commands	**Answer:** *d. ignore commands* The focus word *disobedient* means "not obeying," so a disobedient pet ignores commands. **Reinforcement Activity:** Have students give one or more synonyms of *disobedient*. **Possible Answers:** *naughty, unruly, defiant*
5	**DISAGREE**	Which word does not belong with the others? Tell why it does not belong. disagree argue fight discuss	**Answer:** *discuss*; it does not suggest a difference of opinion. The focus word *disagree* means "to have unlike ideas or opinions." You might ask students to give examples of issues that may trigger disagreement, such as the amount of time they are allowed to spend watching television.

OPTIONAL EXTENSION ACTIVITY

Write the prefix *dis-* on the board. Invite students to find several more words that begin with this prefix, using a dictionary as a resource. Then have students take turns coming to the board and adding the different base words they've found and explaining the meaning of the new words.

Possible Answers: *dislike*—to not like; *disappear*—to stop being visible; *disarm*—to take away weapons; *disorder*—a lack of order; *disconnect*—to break a connection; *disable*—to make unable; *disappoint*—to fail to satisfy the hopes of; *disbelieve*—to consider not true or real; *discourage*—to make less hopeful; *displease*—to make angry

DAY	FOCUS WORD	ACTIVITIES	TEACHER'S NOTES
1	PHOTOGRAPHER	Choose the best word to complete the sentence. A(n) _____ took beautiful snapshots at my sister's wedding. **a.** florist **b.** organist **c.** landscaper **d.** photographer	**Answer:** *d. photographer* The focus word *photographer* means "a person who takes photographs." This word is formed by adding the suffix *-er* to the base word *photograph*. A suffix is a word part added to the end of a word that changes its meaning. The suffixes *-er* and *-or* make words that refer to people engaged in particular activities or occupations.
2	LANDSCAPER	If you were a landscaper, what would you do to turn a vacant lot into a pretty park?	**Possible Answers:** clean it up, plant flowers, make paths, plant bushes, build fountains *Landscaper* means "one who improves the natural beauty of a piece of land." A simple crossword will reinforce the meaning of this focus word. L A N D S C A P E R L A N T B U S H E S
3	DIRECTOR SUPERVISOR	Which word does not belong with the others? director manager supervisor dancer	**Answer:** *dancer*; it does not refer to one who guides others. *Director* means "a person who guides actors and actresses"; *supervisor* means "a person who looks over the work of others." **Reinforcement Activity:** Have students tell how a *director* of a play might help actors and actresses. **Possible Answers:** by helping them speak their lines clearly and use gestures smoothly

DAY	FOCUS WORD	ACTIVITIES	TEACHER'S NOTES
4	EMPLOYER	Which word would be a good substitute for *boss* in the following sentence? When I have a paper route, my boss will be Ms. Sanchez. **a.** worker **b.** assistant **c.** employer **d.** helper	**Answer:** *c. employer* *Employer* means "one who uses the services of others." **Reinforcement Activity:** Have students add the suffixes *-able*, *-ee*, and *-ment* to the base word *employ* and tell the meaning of each word. **Answers:** *employable*—able to be employed; *employee*—a person hired by another; *employment*—work or occupation
5	COUNSELOR	Complete the following analogy: *Counselor* is to *advice* as *doctor* is to _____. counselor : advice :: doctor : _____	**Possible Answers:** *medicine, prescription* The focus word *counselor* means "a person who gives advice." **Reinforcement Activity:** Have students make a word chain by writing in each blank a word that connects to the word that comes before it. *counselor* ➙ *advice* ➙ _____ ➙ _____ ➙ _____ **Possible Answers:** *student, assignment, grade*

OPTIONAL EXTENSION ACTIVITY

Review with students the meaning of the suffixes *-er* and *-or* ("a person who engages"). Have them brainstorm a list of several words that contain these suffixes and that describe people engaged in occupations or actions. List the words on the board. Then have students take turns acting out the words in pantomime while the other students try to guess the words.

Possible Answers: *sailor, singer, batter, runner, skier, skater, dancer, painter, visitor, writer*

Daily Vocabulary   *Level 3*

DAY	FOCUS WORD	ACTIVITIES	TEACHER'S NOTES
1	PENNILESS	Circle the word that means "without money." scoreless shapeless tasteless penniless	**Answer:** *penniless* *Penniless* means "very poor." It is formed by adding the suffix -*less*, which means "without" or "lacking," to the base word *penny*. The *y* changes to *i* when the suffix is added. **Reinforcement Activity:** Discuss the meanings of *scoreless*—without a score; *shapeless*—without shape; *tasteless*—without taste.
2	FEARLESS	Add synonyms to the word web. FEARLESS ⟶ brave	**Possible Answers:** *bold, unafraid, courageous, daring* The focus word *fearless* means "free from fear." You may wish to have students name some occupations that attract fearless people, such as tightrope walking, space travel, firefighting, and law enforcement.
3	HOPELESS	Which word does not belong with the others? hopeless hopeful confident cheerful	**Answer:** *hopeless*; it does not suggest a good outlook. The focus word *hopeless* means "without hope." **Reinforcement Activity:** Have students complete this analogy. *Hopeless* is to *hopeful* as _____ is to *nearby*. **Possible Answers:** *far, distant*

DAY	FOCUS WORD	ACTIVITIES	TEACHER'S NOTES
4	WORTHLESS	Complete the following analogy: *Worthless* is to _____ as *selfish* is to *generous*. worthless : _____ :: selfish : generous	**Possible Answers:** *valuable, useful, excellent* The focus word *worthless* means "lacking worth." **Reinforcement Activity:** Have students unscramble the letters to find a word that is an antonym of *worthless*. pcerisuo **Answer:** *precious*

5	HEARTLESS	Which character is heartless?
		
		  a. Aladdin
		  b. Peter Pan
		  c. Snow White's stepmother
		  d. Belle in *Beauty and the Beast*
			Answer: *c. Snow White's stepmother*
			
			The focus word *heartless* means "unfeeling" or "cruel."
			
			Reinforcement Activity: Have students give one or more antonyms of *heartless*.
			
			Possible Answers: *kind, considerate, sympathetic, sensitive*

OPTIONAL EXTENSION ACTIVITY

The suffix *-less* means "without." Invite students to find five more words that end with this suffix. Ask them to tell the meaning of each word.

Possible Answers: *sleeveless*—without sleeves; *useless*—without use or worth; *changeless*—without change; *careless*—without care or thought; *defenseless*—without protection

Daily Vocabulary   Level 3

DAY	FOCUS WORD	ACTIVITIES	TEACHER'S NOTES
1	**DREADFUL**	Which "word math" problem creates a word that means "horrible" or "terrible"? delight + ful = sorrow + ful = dread + ful = wonder + ful =	**Answer:** *dread + ful =* The focus word *dreadful* means "causing great fear." The word is formed by adding the suffix *-ful*, which means "full of or characterized by," to the base word dread. **Reinforcement Activity:** Have students give one or more synonyms of *dreadful*. **Possible Answers:** *scary, frightful, awful*
2	**PLENTIFUL**	Which phrase means the same as the word *plentiful* in the following sentence? The rich soil and gentle rain produced a plentiful harvest. **a.** full of insects **b.** in great demand **c.** in large supply **d.** in the usual way	**Answer:** *c. in large supply* The focus word *plentiful* means "abundant; more than enough." The letter y in the word *plenty* changes to *i* when the suffix *-ful* is added. **Reinforcement Activity:** Have students unscramble the following letters to find an antonym of *plentiful*. sacecr **Answer:** *scarce*
3	**HURTFUL** **MERCIFUL**	Which word does not belong with the others? Tell why it does not belong. hurtful kind forgiving merciful gentle	**Answer:** *hurtful*; it does not mean "sensitive to others." The focus words have opposite meanings. *Hurtful* means "causing injury." *Merciful* means "giving kind treatment." **Reinforcement Activity:** Ask students to name actions that they consider hurtful to their classmates. **Possible Answers:** saying mean things to them, calling them names, not letting them play a game

DAY	FOCUS WORD	ACTIVITIES	TEACHER'S NOTES
4	MOURNFUL	In the following sentence, replace the word *sad* with a more descriptive synonym. The funeral of President Kennedy was a sad event. **a.** public **b.** televised **c.** joyful **d.** mournful	**Answer:** *d. mournful* The focus word *mournful* means "full of sorrow," and therefore can replace the word *sad*. **Reinforcement Activity:** Have students complete this analogy: *Mournful* is to *grief* as _____ is to *joy* **Possible Answers:** *happy, joyful, glad*
5	EVENTFUL	Choose the best word to complete the sentence. The _____ afternoon included a trip to the zoo, a visit to the gift shop, and a ride on a pony. **a.** eventful **b.** dull **c.** ordinary **d.** boring	**Answer:** *a. eventful* The phrases "a trip to the zoo," "a visit to the gift shop," and "a ride on a pony" provide context clues to the meaning of *eventful*, which means "filled with events." You may wish to have students describe eventful days that they have experienced.

OPTIONAL EXTENSION ACTIVITY

Have students list several words containing the suffix *-ful*, such as *wonderful, truthful, graceful, painful, playful, skillful,* and *shameful*. Then have students sort the words into two groups: those describing positive qualities and those describing negative qualities. Make a chart of these words on the board, starting with the words presented in this lesson.

Possible Answers:

Positive	Negative
merciful	dreadful
plentiful	hurtful
eventful	painful
wonderful	

DAY	FOCUS WORD	ACTIVITIES	TEACHER'S NOTES
1	**MILEAGE**	Choose the phrase that best completes the sentence. If a car has high mileage, it must _____. **a.** have had several owners **b.** be very old **c.** have many dents and scratches **d.** have been driven a lot	**Answer:** *d. have been driven a lot* The focus word *mileage* means "distance expressed in miles." **Reinforcement Activity:** Have students explain why choices *a*, *b*, and *c* wouldn't necessarily be true. **Possible Answer:** A car with high mileage may have had one owner and may have no dents. It may also have been driven a great deal in a short time.
2	**CIRCUMFERENCE**	Choose the best word to complete the sentence. The _____ of the earth, or the distance around it, is approximately 25,000 miles at the equator. **a.** speed **b.** circumference **c.** orbit **d.** gravity	**Answer:** *b. circumference* The phrase "the distance around it" provides a context clue to the meaning of *circumference*, which means "the distance around something." You may choose to have students measure the circumferences of several objects, such as a classroom globe, a baseball, a basketball, a beach ball, a soccer ball, and maybe their own heads.
3	**METER** **KILOMETER**	Complete the following analogy: *Meter* is to *kilometer* as *foot* is to _____. meter : kilometer :: foot : _____	**Possible Answer:** *mile* A meter is equal to about 39.37 inches. It is the basic unit of length in the metric system. A kilometer equals 1,000 meters.

Daily Vocabulary

Level 3

DAY	FOCUS WORD	ACTIVITIES	TEACHER'S NOTES
4	SQUARE FOOT	10 ft. / 8 ft. (rectangle) This room has an area of 80 _____.	**Answer:** *square feet* A square foot is a unit of area equal to the area of a square measuring one foot by one foot. **Reinforcement Activity:** Have students look around the classroom and name some objects that can be measured in square feet. **Possible Answers:** ceiling, floor, walls, panes of glass, maps, screens
5	ACRE	Who do you think has more land—someone who owns 100 square feet of land or someone who owns 100 acres of land?	**Answer:** someone who owns 100 acres An acre is a measure of land equal to 43,560 square feet, so 100 acres equals 4,356,000 square feet of land. Tell students to picture an acre of land as a little smaller than a football field.

OPTIONAL EXTENSION ACTIVITY

Have students brainstorm three things that might be measured in each of the following units: kilometers, square feet, acres.

Possible Answers: kilometers—roads, railroad tracks, and bike paths; square feet—carpets, walls, and lawns; acres—farms, housing lots, and golf courses

DAY	FOCUS WORD	ACTIVITIES	TEACHER'S NOTES
1	**MULTIPLY**	Choose the correct word to complete the sentence. If you _____ 3 by 7, your answer is 21. **a.** add **b.** subtract **c.** multiply **d.** divide	**Answer:** *c. multiply* The focus word *multiply* means "to find the product of two or more numbers." Ask students to explain the relationship between addition and multiplication. **Reinforcement Activity:** Have students multiply these pairs of numbers: 2 and 4, 3 and 5, 6 and 5, 7 and 6. **Answers:** 8, 15, 30, 42
2	**PRODUCT**	In the problem below, which number is the product? $$\begin{array}{r} 9 \\ \times\,7 \\ \hline 63 \end{array}$$	**Answer:** *63* The focus word *product* means "the number obtained by multiplying two or more numbers." **Reinforcement Activity:** Have students multiply 9 by a number from 1 to 10. Then have them add the two digits in the product. Ask students to identify the answer they always get. **Answer:** 9
3	**GRAPH**	What would you call the kind of picture shown below? What information is it giving? **Andrea's Basketball Scores** 	**Answers:** *The picture is a graph; it shows how many points Andrea scored on each of the five days.* The focus word *graph* means "a diagram or chart that presents information." Ask students how they can find out the number of points Andrea scored each day. Then ask students to name the day on which Andrea scored the most points (*Monday*) and the day on which she scored the fewest points (*Thursday*).

DAY	FOCUS WORD	ACTIVITIES	TEACHER'S NOTES
4	ESTIMATE	Which word would be a good substitute for *guessed* in the following sentence?　Before counting the pennies in the jar, I guessed the total number.　**a.** multiplied　**b.** subtracted　**c.** estimated　**d.** added	**Answer:** *c. estimated*　The focus word *estimate* means "to form a rough idea of the value, size, or cost of something."　**Reinforcement Activity:** Ask students to name things that a person might estimate.　**Possible Answers:** the number of people in a crowd, the answer to a math problem, a person's height or weight, the total cost of two or more items in a store
5	CALCULATE	Add related words to the word web. add CALCULATE	**Possible Answers:** *subtract, multiply, estimate*　The focus word *calculate* means "to find by adding, subtracting, multiplying, or dividing."　**Reinforcement Activity:** Ask students to name a machine that people use to calculate answers to mathematical problems (**Possible Answer:** *calculator*). You may wish to give students some equations, such as 23 + 37 = ___ and 12 x 12 = ___, to solve with a calculator.

OPTIONAL EXTENSION ACTIVITY

Have each student create a math problem using one of the week's vocabulary words *(multiply, product, graph, estimate, calculate)* for an imaginary math test. Explain to students that they should create a problem that they themselves can solve. After all students have created problems, have the class discuss several of them, including how they can be solved.

Sample Problem: *Sam read 4 books each week for 4 weeks. How many books did he read?*

Solution: *Multiply the number of books by the number of weeks to get 16 books for the answer.*

Daily Vocabulary

Level 3

DAY	FOCUS WORD	ACTIVITIES	TEACHER'S NOTES
1	**DIVIDEND**	What if 2 friends wanted to share 24 comic books equally? Write a division problem that shows how many comic books each friend would get. Label the dividend.	**Answer:** $24 \div 2 = 12$; *24 is the dividend* The focus word *dividend* means "a number to be divided by another number." **Reinforcement Activity:** Have students supply the missing dividend in each of the following equations: ___ $\div 4 = 6$ ___ $\div 3 = 9$ ___ $\div 2 = 5$ **Answers:** 24, 27, 10

2	**DIVISOR**	Choose the best word to complete the following sentence:
		
		    When you divide 12 by 4, the number 4 is called the _____.
		
		    a. divisor
		    b. sum
		    c. dividend
		    d. product
			Answer: *a. divisor*
			
			The focus word *divisor* means "the number by which a dividend is divided."
			
			Reinforcement Activity: Have students supply the missing divisor in each of the following equations:
			
			$50 \div$ ___ $= 1$, $50 \div$ ___ $= 2$, $50 \div$ ___ $= 5$
			
			Answers: 50, 25, 10

3	**QUOTIENT**	Complete the following analogy:
		
		    Division is to *quotient* as *addition* is to _____.
		
		    division : quotient :: addition : _____
			Possible Answers: *sum, total*
			
			The focus word *quotient* means "the number obtained by dividing one number by another."
			
			Reinforcement Activity: Ask students to find the quotient in each of these equations:
			
			$16 \div 2 =$ ___ $24 \div 4 =$ ___ $35 \div 5 =$ ___
			
			Answers: 8, 6, 7

DAY	FOCUS WORD	ACTIVITIES	TEACHER'S NOTES
4	AVERAGE	What is the *average* number of blocks in these towers?	**Answer:** 4 An *average* is the value reached after "evening out" several numbers. An average can be found by adding quantities together and dividing by their number. **Reinforcement Activity:** Find the average score of a baseball team that scored 5 runs in game one, 0 runs in game two, and 7 runs in game three. **Answer:** 4
5	FRACTION	Draw a picture for each fraction. Start with a circle. ◯ $\frac{1}{2}$ $\frac{1}{4}$ $\frac{3}{4}$	**Possible Answers:** ◐ ⊕ ⊕ The focus word *fraction* means "a number, such as $\frac{1}{2}$ or $\frac{2}{3}$, that indicates one or more equal parts of a whole." **Reinforcement Activity:** Have students name activities that require the use of fractions. **Possible Answers:** cooking, sewing, model building

OPTIONAL EXTENSION ACTIVITY

Ask students to make up division word problems for one another to solve. Ask them to state their problems in this way: "The dividend is 100. The divisor is 50. What is the quotient?"

Daily Vocabulary

DAY	FOCUS WORD	ACTIVITIES	TEACHER'S NOTES
1	**ENCHANT**	Which word does not belong with the others? Tell why it does not belong. magician guard enchant witch spell	**Answer:** *guard;* it has nothing to do with magic. The focus word *enchant* means "to put under a spell as if by charms or magic." **Reinforcement Activity:** Ask students to name enchanted characters in stories they have heard or read. **Possible Answers:** Snow White, the Frog Prince, Sleeping Beauty
2	**TRANSFORM**	What does Cinderella's fairy godmother transform a pumpkin into?	**Answer:** a coach The focus word *transform* means "to change completely." **Reinforcement Activity:** Nature will transform each of the following into something else: an egg, a caterpillar, a tadpole, a seed. Ask students to tell what each will become. **Possible Answers:** egg—bird, chicken; caterpillar—butterfly, moth; tadpole—frog; seed—plant
3	**OGRE**	What does the word *ogre* mean in the following sentence? The ogre's huge size, ugly appearance, and mean acts made everyone in the village fear him. **a.** an elf **b.** a fairy princess **c.** a magic fish **d.** an ugly giant	**Answer:** *d. an ugly giant* The focus word *ogre* means "an ugly giant of fairy tales and folk tales." Point out the context clues in the sentence ("huge size," "ugly appearance," "mean acts"). **Reinforcement Activity:** Ask students to suggest other words to describe an ogre. **Possible Answers:** *cruel, wicked, large, bad*

DAY	FOCUS WORD	ACTIVITIES	TEACHER'S NOTES
4	OUTWIT	Give a synonym for the word *outwit* in the following sentence: Hansel and Gretel managed to outwit the witch who had captured them.	**Possible Answers:** *fool, outsmart* The focus word *outwit* means "to get the better of by cleverness." **Reinforcement Activity:** Ask students to name characters who have outwitted other characters in books, television shows, or films. **Possible Answers:** the three little pigs, the roadrunner, Jack in "Jack and the Beanstalk"

5	MYSTERIOUS	Which place would most likely be described as mysterious?
		
		  a. a village fair
		  b. a palace
		  c. a deserted old house
		  d. a garden
			Answer: *c. a deserted old house*
			
			The focus word *mysterious* means "strange; unusual; hard to understand." The letter *y* in the word *mystery* changes to *i* when the suffix *-ous* is added.
			
			Reinforcement Activity: Ask students to describe mysterious characters and places in stories they know.

OPTIONAL EXTENSION ACTIVITY

Have the class name folk tales and fairy tales they know. Then have them take turns making up sentences that describe events in those tales. Each sentence should contain one of the words in this week's list.

Possible Answer: In "The Frog Prince," a handsome prince is transformed into an ugly frog.

DAY	FOCUS WORD	ACTIVITIES	TEACHER'S NOTES
1	LEGEND	Which word does not belong with the others? story tale legend painting	**Answer:** *painting;* it does not describe something told in words. The focus word *legend* means "an old story that many people believe but that cannot be proved true." *Legend, story,* and *tale* are similar in meaning. **Reinforcement Activity:** You may wish to have students give some examples of legends, such as those about Robin Hood, William Tell, and King Arthur.
2	MYTH	What does *myth* mean in the following sentence? One famous myth tells the story of Hercules, who strangled two snakes in his cradle.	**Possible Answer:** a story about someone more than human A *myth* is a story that tells about a superhuman being, often in order to explain something in nature. You may choose to retell a famous myth, such as that of Echo and Narcissus or that of Demeter and Persephone.
3	FABLE	Which of these stories is not a fable? **a.** "The Ant and the Grasshopper" **b.** "The Tortoise and the Hare" **c.** *Charlotte's Web* **d.** "The Fox and the Crow"	**Answer:** *c. Charlotte's Web* The focus word *fable* means "a brief story, usually with animal characters, that teaches a lesson." **Reinforcement Activity:** Have students present short skits in which they role-play characters from fables they have heard, such as the town mouse and the country mouse or the ant and the grasshopper.

DAY	FOCUS WORD	ACTIVITIES	TEACHER'S NOTES
4	FANTASY	Make a word chain. In each blank write a word or phrase that connects to the one that comes before or after it. _____ → _____ → *fantasy* → *The Wizard of Oz* → _____ → _____ → _____ → _____	**Possible Answers:** story, imagination, Dorothy, dancing scarecrow, wicked witch, magic slippers A *fantasy* is a story set in an imaginary world. **Reinforcement Activity:** Ask students how a fantasy is different from a news story. **Possible Answer:** A fantasy tells about impossible people and events; a news story tells about real people and events.
5	TALL TALE	In what kind of story would you likely find the following details? When Paul Bunyan was a baby, he was so big that he outgrew his house. His family put him in a floating cradle. It took a tidal wave to rock his cradle. **a.** legend **c.** fable **b.** myth **d.** tall tale	**Answer:** *d. tall tale* A tall tale is a story that exaggerates or stretches the facts, so details about the great size of Paul Bunyan would be found in this kind of story. **Reinforcement Activity:** Encourage students to create other exaggerations for a tall tale about Paul Bunyan. **Possible Answer:** Paul Bunyan once chopped down a grove of trees with a single swing of his mighty ax.

OPTIONAL EXTENSION ACTIVITY

Have students create a chart, using this week's focus words as headings. Have them complete the chart with the words and phrases below. Some items can be used in more than one column. lesson, talking animals, superhumans, brave men and women, a woman who can leap a mile, dogs with bank accounts, how seasons came to be, a ten-foot-tall man, people with three eyes, tests of courage

Possible Answers:

Legend	brave men and women, tests of courage
Myth	how seasons came to be, superhumans
Tall Tale	a woman who can leap a mile, a ten-foot tall man
Fantasy	dogs with bank accounts, people with three eyes
Fable	lesson, talking animals

Daily Vocabulary *Level 3*

DAY	FOCUS WORD	ACTIVITIES	TEACHER'S NOTES
1	**FICTION** **NONFICTION**	Arrange the following titles in the chart below: *The Secret Garden, The Life of Dr. Martin Luther King, Jr., Alice in Wonderland, The Wizard of Oz.* <table><tr><td>**FICTION**</td><td>**NONFICTION**</td></tr><tr><td></td><td></td></tr></table>	**Answer:** fiction—*The Secret Garden, Alice in Wonderland, The Wizard of Oz;* nonfiction—*The Life of Dr. Martin Luther King, Jr.* *Fiction* means "a made-up story." *Nonfiction* means "writings that are based on truth," such as biographies and news stories. Call upon students to mention details that are made-up in works of fiction that they have read.
2	**EVENT**	Add one or more events to the following story: Maraya found the wounded bird. It had crashed against the window. One of its wings was broken.	**Possible Answer:** Maraya lifted the bird and cradled it in her hands. Gently she carried it into the house. The focus word *event* means "something that happens in a story." **Reinforcement Activity:** Have students continue adding events to the story about Maraya and the wounded bird.
3	**PLOT**	Complete the following analogy: *Plot* is to *events* as *puzzle* is to _____. plot : events :: puzzle : _____	**Possible Answer:** *pieces* *Plot* means "the series of events in a story." Just as a puzzle consists of separate pieces that form a whole, a plot consists of separate events that form a story. **Reinforcement Activity:** Have students imagine that they are going to write a mystery story. Then ask them to describe an event that might begin the plot. **Possible Answers:** A stranger knocks at midnight; an eerie light suddenly glows in an old house.

DAY	FOCUS WORD	ACTIVITIES	TEACHER'S NOTES
4	CHARACTER	List the characters from your favorite TV show or movie.	**Answer:** Any answer that students can support with examples is acceptable. *Character* means "a person in a story or play." You may choose to point out some of the ways in which writers reveal the qualities of their characters, such as by describing the characters' appearance or by presenting the characters' speech, thoughts, feelings, and actions.
5	SETTING	Imagine you are writing a story about a girl who survives a plane crash in the Arctic. What would you not include in the setting of this story? **a.** igloos and glaciers **b.** wolves, reindeer, and moose **c.** cold weather **d.** fields of waving corn	**Answer:** *d. fields of waving corn* *Setting* means "the time and place of the action of a story or play." In the arctic setting of this story, details about fields of waving corn are out of place. **Reinforcement Activity:** Have students suggest details for settings in a jungle (tigers, quicksand, trees); a farm (silo, cow, barn); a ranch (horses, corral, bunkhouse).

OPTIONAL EXTENSION ACTIVITY

Have students invent a story as a group. First, divide the class into three groups and assign one group to create characters, another to describe a setting, and the third to list the events of a plot. Then have one member of each group report what the group has created. Finally, have the groups combine their elements of plot, setting, and character to create a written or oral story. Alternatively, the class could be divided into groups of three students, with each group inventing its own characters, setting, and events.

Daily Vocabulary   Level 3

DAY	FOCUS WORD	ACTIVITIES	TEACHER'S NOTES
1	SITAR	Which would not be part of a sitar? a. strings b. keyboard c. wooden neck d. frets	**Answer:** *b. keyboard* The focus word *sitar* refers to a stringed instrument of India. A sitar has a long wooden neck, a pear-shaped body made from a gourd, and seven main strings. For this word and the others in this lesson, you may want to play a recording of music that features each instrument.
2	MARIMBA	What does the word *marimba* mean in the following sentence? Several musicians struck the bars of the marimba, producing a rich sound.	**Answer:** The focus word *marimba* means "an instrument that looks like a xylophone." A marimba has a number of bars arranged on a frame, like the keys of a piano. These bars are struck with a mallet. Point out that marimbas are often heard in African and Caribbean music.
3	MARACA	Complete the following analogy. *Beat* is to *drum* as _____ is to *maraca*. beat : drum :: _____ : maraca	**Answers:** *shake* The focus word *maraca* means "a rattle made from a gourd with seeds or pebbles inside." Maracas are usually shaken in pairs to beat out a rhythm. **Reinforcement Activity:** Have students complete the following chain. Latin music → maraca → ____ → ____ → ____ → ____ **Possible Answers:** *rattle, shake, beat, rhythm*

DAY	FOCUS WORD	ACTIVITIES	TEACHER'S NOTES
4	GONG	Match the instrument to the part used to play it. gong bow violin stick drum mallet	**Answers:** gong—mallet; violin—bow; drum—stick The focus word *gong* means "a metallic disk that produces a ringing tone." A gong hangs on a stand and is struck with a mallet. **Reinforcement Activity:** Ask students to name another instrument that produces a ringing tone. **Possible Answer:** cymbal
5	MANDOLIN	Which word does not belong with the others? Tell why it does not belong. mandolin guitar sitar banjo trumpet	**Answer:** *trumpet;* it is not the name of a stringed instrument. The focus word *mandolin* means "a small instrument with four to six pairs of strings played by plucking." The mandolin is often heard in country and bluegrass bands, along with the banjo and the guitar.

OPTIONAL EXTENSION ACTIVITY

Invite students to work in small groups to research an instrument mentioned in this week's lesson, an instrument they play, or one they are curious about. Have each group create a poster presenting the information they find.

Daily Vocabulary   Level 3

DAY	FOCUS WORD	ACTIVITIES	TEACHER'S NOTES
1	MURAL FRESCO	Choose the correct ending to complete the sentence. If an artist has painted a mural or a fresco, you would probably find it on a _____. **a.** teacup **b.** package of cereal **c.** wall **d.** statue	**Answer:** *c. wall* Both focus words describe paintings usually found on walls. The word *mural* means "a painting on a wall," and *fresco* means "a painting made on wet plaster." You may choose to have students look up information about Diego Rivera, a twentieth-century artist who revived the art of fresco painting in Mexico.
2	PORTRAIT	Whose portrait is on a five-dollar bill?	**Answer:** Abraham Lincoln's The focus word *portrait* means "a picture of a person, usually showing the face." You may want to point out that portraits can be either paintings or photographs. **Reinforcement Activity:** Have students name other items on which portraits of famous people can be found. **Possible Answers:** stamps, coins, baseball cards

3	CANVAS	What would you not expect to find in a painter's workplace?
		
		    a. paint
		    b. brushes
		    c. canvas
		    d. electric drill
			Answer: *d. electric drill;* it is not used in a painter's work.
			
			The focus word *canvas* means "a special cloth on which oil paintings are made."
			
			Reinforcement Activity: Have students complete the following word chain:
			
			artist ➜ canvas ➜ _____ ➜ _____ ➜ _____
			
			Possible Answers: *oil paints, painting, portrait*

DAY	FOCUS WORD	ACTIVITIES	TEACHER'S NOTES
4	EASEL	Correct the errors in the following chart: **ARTIST** — paints, brushes / canvas / music stand **MUSICIAN** — instrument / sheet music / easel	**Answer:** *Music stand* and *easel* should switch columns. The focus word *easel* means "an upright frame for holding an artist's work." **Reinforcement Activity:** The word *easel* comes from a Dutch word meaning "donkey." Ask students to explain how an easel is like a donkey. **Possible Answer:** Both an easel and a donkey can "carry" things.
5	PALETTE	If you were painting a picture of a circus, what colors would you select from your palette, and why?	**Answer:** Accept any answer students can support. The focus word *palette* means "a thin board or tablet on which a painter puts and mixes colors." **Reinforcement Activity:** Ask students to identify the word that does not belong. painter palette photograph canvas easel **Answer:** *photograph*

The chart in the activity:

ARTIST	MUSICIAN
paints, brushes	instrument
canvas	sheet music
music stand	easel

OPTIONAL EXTENSION ACTIVITY

Ask students to bring to class some of their own sketches and drawings and any watercolor or oil paintings they may have done. Have students show their work to their classmates. Students might also bring to class reproductions of paintings and tell what they like about their favorite ones. If possible, invite a local artist to speak to the class and display paintings to the students.

DAY	FOCUS WORD	ACTIVITIES	TEACHER'S NOTES
1	**CHORUS**	Choose the word that best completes the sentence. If you join a chorus, you can expect to do a lot of _____. **a.** debating **b.** acting **c.** writing **d.** singing	**Answer:** *d. singing* The focus word *chorus* means "a group of singers." **Reinforcement Activity:** Have students unscramble the following letters to make a word that is a synonym of chorus: hcrio **Answer:** *choir*
2	**DUET** **TRIO** **QUARTET**	Match each group of performers with the correct number. <table><tr><td>**Performers**</td><td>**Number**</td></tr><tr><td>duet</td><td>3</td></tr><tr><td>quartet</td><td>4</td></tr><tr><td>trio</td><td>2</td></tr></table>	**Answer:** duet—2; trio—3; quartet—4 *Duet, trio,* and *quartet* come from Italian and refer to groups of two, three, and four performers respectively, or to musical compositions written for these numbers of performers. Spanish-speaking students may notice similarities between these words and the Spanish words for two, three, and four: *dos, tres,* and *cuatro.*
3	**ALTO** **SOPRANO**	What do the words *alto* and *soprano* mean in the following sentence? My sister, who sings low notes beautifully, is an alto, not a soprano.	**Answer:** The words *alto* and *soprano* usually refer to female singers. An alto has the lowest female singing voice; a soprano, the highest one. Students should use context clues to help them identify the meanings of the words. The clause "who sings low notes beautifully" provides a clue to the meaning of *alto;* the word *not* signals the contrast between *alto* and *soprano.*

DAY	FOCUS WORD	ACTIVITIES	TEACHER'S NOTES

4	**TENOR**
	
	BASS
		Which word does not belong with the others? Tell why it does not belong.
		
		    alto soprano tenor bass microphone
			Answer: *microphone;* it does not refer to a singer.
			
			Tenor and *bass* refer to male singers. A tenor has the highest male singing voice; a bass has the lowest one.
			
			Reinforcement Activity: Have students complete this analogy:
			
			    Bass is to *tenor* as *alto* is to _____.
			
			Answer: *soprano*

5	**BARITONE**	Arrange the following words for male singing voices on the scale below.
		
		    tenor
		    bass
		    baritone ├────┼────┤
		            low middle high
			Answer: low—bass; middle—baritone; high—tenor
			
			The focus word *baritone* means "a male singer with a voice in the middle range, between tenor and bass."
			
			Reinforcement Activity: Have students complete this analogy:
			
			    Baritone is to *singer* as *drum* is to _____.
			
			Possible Answer: *instrument*

OPTIONAL EXTENSION ACTIVITY

This lesson provides a fine opportunity to combine music appreciation and vocabulary building. Invite students to bring to class cassette recordings of popular singers. After each recording is played, have students identify the singer's type of voice, using words from this week's lesson. You may wish to play recordings made by classical artists to broaden students' listening experiences.

Daily Vocabulary   *Level* **3**

DAY	FOCUS WORD	ACTIVITIES	TEACHER'S NOTES
1	**PERFORMANCE**	Which word does not belong with the others? Tell why it does not belong. performance concert opera circus stage	**Answer:** *stage;* it does not refer to a presentation before an audience. The focus word *performance* means "a public entertainment." **Reinforcement Activity:** Ask students to name performances they have either seen or been a part of.
2	**REHEARSE**	Complete the following analogy: *Rehearse* is to *play* as _____ is to *test.* rehearse : play :: _____ : test	**Answer:** *study* The word *rehearse* means "to practice in preparation for a public performance." You rehearse to prepare for a play, and you study to prepare for a test. **Reinforcement Activity:** Ask students what the practice session for a public performance is called. **Answer:** a rehearsal
3	**UNDERSTUDY**	In which of the following situations would an understudy be asked to perform? **a.** The script needs to be rewritten. **b.** The director of the play decides to quit. **c.** The stage lights are not working properly. **d.** An actor becomes ill on the night of the performance.	**Answer:** *d. An actor becomes ill on the night of the performance.* The focus word *understudy* means "an actor who is prepared to take over another actor's part if necessary." Ask students to identify the two words that form *understudy* (*under* and *study*). Point out that an understudy learns the part of another actor to serve as a substitute in an emergency.

DAY	FOCUS WORD	ACTIVITIES	TEACHER'S NOTES
4	**SKIT**	Choose the best word to complete the following sentence: The campers presented a short _____ in which they acted like their counselors. **a.** opera **b.** award **c.** skit **d.** speech	**Answer:** *c. skit* Point out that the context clues "presented," "short," and "in which they acted like their counselors" suggest that the answer must be *skit*, which means "a brief, funny play."
5	**DIALOGUE**	Which one of the following usually does not include dialogue? Explain why. **a.** a movie **b.** a concert **c.** a skit **d.** a book	**Answer:** *b. a concert*; it is a musical performance. The focus word *dialogue* means "a conversation between two or more people." You may wish to remind students that dialogue can be spoken or written. **Reinforcement Activity:** Ask students how dialogue can be recognized in written works. **Answer:** The words of the characters are inside quotation marks.

OPTIONAL EXTENSION ACTIVITY

Divide students into small groups and have each group create a skit to perform for the class. A group may choose a brief familiar story, such as a fable, or an episode from a book or movie, or they may invent a story of their own. Have each group hold at least one rehearsal.

Daily Vocabulary   *Level* **3**

DAY	FOCUS WORD	ACTIVITIES	TEACHER'S NOTES
1	**HARDWARE**	What different meanings does the word *hardware* have in the following sentences? I bought an electric drill for Mom at the hardware store. We saw such hardware as monitors and printers at the new computer superstore.	**Answer:** In the first sentence, *hardware* means "articles made of metal, such as tools, nails, and utensils." In the second sentence, *hardware* means "the physical equipment that makes up a computer." **Reinforcement Activity:** Have students point out pieces of computer hardware in your classroom or school learning center.
2	**KEYBOARD**	Which word would be a good substitute for the underlined phrase in the following sentence? It took me about a week to learn the <u>rows of letters and numbers</u> on that computer. **a.** dials **b.** keyboard **c.** letters **d.** dashboard	**Answer:** *b. keyboard* The word *keyboard* means "the rows of keys of a computer." If you wish, point out the rows of letters, numbers, and symbols on a real computer keyboard. **Reinforcement Activity:** Have students name other objects that may be operated with a keyboard. **Possible Answers:** a piano, a typewriter, a telephone
3	**SCREEN**	Choose the correct word to complete the sentence. The little man jumped out of the way of the dragon on my computer _____. **a.** screen **b.** keyboard **c.** keys **d.** list	**Answer:** *a. screen* The word *screen* means "the part of the computer on which pictures and text appear." **Reinforcement Activity:** Have students discuss what they can do to the text and images on a computer screen. **Possible Answers:** change them, control them

DAY	FOCUS WORD	ACTIVITIES	TEACHER'S NOTES
4	MENU	What different meanings does the word *menu* have in these two sentences? My father ordered his favorite dinner from the restaurant menu. I chose the edit function from the menu shown on my computer screen.	**Answer:** In the first sentence, *menu* means "a list of dishes available for a meal." In the second sentence, *menu* means "a list of functions displayed on the screen of a computer." In the first sentence, point out the context clue "ordered his favorite dinner." In the second sentence, point out the clues "edit function" and "shown on my computer screen."
5	COMMAND	Choose the correct answer. If you want a computer to perform a certain function, you give it a _____. **a.** memo **b.** polite request **c.** command **d.** shove	**Answer:** *c. command* The focus word *command* means "a single instruction that a computer follows immediately." **Reinforcement Activity:** Ask students to suggest some commands that they might give a computer. **Possible Answers:** open, print, enter

OPTIONAL EXTENSION ACTIVITY

Have students play the game "buzz." Each student should silently choose a computer word and make up a sentence that contains the word. Have students take turns saying their sentences aloud, substituting *buzz* for the chosen word so that the other students can try to guess the word that belongs in the sentence. Discuss any reasonable response, even if it is not the answer that the speaker intended.

Daily Vocabulary *Level 3*

DAY	FOCUS WORD	ACTIVITIES	TEACHER'S NOTES
1	DATA	Match each word on the left with its meaning on the right. menu — a single instruction that a computer follows immediately data — a list of computer functions command — information	**Answer:** menu—a list of computer functions; data—information; command—a single instruction that a computer follows immediately Point out to students that a computer can work with data, or information, but cannot gather it. Humans have to gather the data that the computer uses when it calculates or sorts information.
2	PROGRAM	What two different meanings does the word *program* have in these two sentences? I watch my favorite television program every Tuesday evening. My computer has a program for creating pictures.	**Answer:** In the first sentence, *program* means "a scheduled broadcast." In the second sentence, *program* means "a set of instructions that tell a computer what to do to complete a task." **Reinforcement Activity:** Ask students what a person who creates computer programs is called. **Answer:** a programmer
3	DISK	What does the word *disk* mean in the following sentence? Sasha slid the disk into her computer and opened the file called "Whales."	**Answer:** a thin, flat plate on which computer data and programs can be stored Point out the context clues "into her computer" and "opened the file called 'Whales.'" **Reinforcement Activity:** Ask students to suggest other things that store information. **Possible Answers:** books, videotapes, CD's, audiotapes

DAY	FOCUS WORD	ACTIVITIES	TEACHER'S NOTES
4	SOFTWARE	Which of the following is an example of computer software? **a.** a computer game **b.** a computer monitor **c.** a computer printer **d.** a computer keyboard	**Answer:** *a. a computer game* The focus word *software* means "the programs used by a computer to perform tasks." **Reinforcement Activity:** Have students name examples of computer software that they have used.
5	MOUSE	What different meanings does the word *mouse* have in these two sentences? Have you see Squeaky, my pet mouse? By moving the mouse with her hand, Mona selected a drawing tool on the computer screen.	**Answer:** In the first sentence, *mouse* refers to a small furry animal. In the second sentence, *mouse* means "a small hand-held device that allows a user to control a computer." If possible, have a student point out a computer mouse in your classroom or school learning center. That student might also demonstrate its use.

OPTIONAL EXTENSION ACTIVITY

Suggest that students become word detectives, looking for this week's and last week's computer words in newspapers, magazines, catalogs, and books. Have students copy the sentences in which the words appear and share the words they find. Afterward, you may wish to collect students' sentences and use them in a bulletin-board display entitled "Computer Words in Print."

Daily Vocabulary Level **3**

DAY	FOCUS WORD	ACTIVITIES	TEACHER'S NOTES
1	**BRAILLE**	Choose the correct answer. In what alphabet is the word *and* written in rows of raised dots like this? ● ● ● ● ● ● ● ● **a.** cursive **b.** French **c.** braille **d.** Greek	**Answer:** *c. braille* The focus word *braille* means "a system of printing for the blind in which letters are represented by groups of raised dots." The braille alphabet was invented by Louis Braille, a blind Frenchman who taught blind children about 150 years ago. The braille system is based on an arrangement of six raised dots used in 63 combinations.
2	**GUPPY**	Complete the following analogy: *Dalmation* is to *dog* as *guppy* is to _____. dalmation : dog :: guppy : _____	**Answer:** *fish* A dalmation is a type of dog, and a guppy is a type of fish. The focus word *guppy* means "a small tropical minnow often kept as an aquarium fish." The word comes from the name R. J. L. Guppy, who first provided specimens of this fish for the British Museum. **Reinforcement Activity:** Ask students to name other kinds of fish. **Possible Answers:** trout, goldfish, carp, bass
3	**LEOTARD**	What error do you see in the word web below? acrobat — LEOTARD — gymnast surgeon — LEOTARD — dancer	**Answer:** *Surgeon* does not belong because a surgeon does not wear a leotard while at work. *Leotard* means "a tight, one-piece garment worn by dancers and acrobats." Jules Léotard, a French acrobat, made the leotard popular in France. **Reinforcement Activity:** Have students complete this analogy: *Leotard* is to *dancer* as _____ is to *knight.* **Possible Answer:** *armor*

DAY	FOCUS WORD	ACTIVITIES	TEACHER'S NOTES
4	ATLAS	Match the item with the book that contains it. definition of braille encyclopedia map of India dictionary article about guppies atlas	**Answers:** *definition of braille—dictionary; map of India—atlas; article about guppies—encyclopedia* The focus word *atlas* means "a book of maps." The word *atlas* comes from the name of a Titan in Greek mythology who supported the heavens on his shoulders.
5	DENIM	What word does not belong with the others? Tell why it does not belong. wool denim plastic flannel cotton	**Answer:** *plastic*; it is not a fabric. The focus word *denim* means "a firm, often coarse, cloth, used for making jeans and overalls." The word comes from the French phrase *serge de Nîmes*. Serge is a strong cloth, and Nîmes is a city in France where much of that cloth was made during the time of the Roman Empire.

OPTIONAL EXTENSION ACTIVITY

Tell students that several words made from names have entered our language, and it can be interesting to explore connections between the word and the name it comes from. Have students work in small groups to complete the following chart. Students may use a dictionary or an encyclopedia if they wish.

Name	Clue	Word
Adolphe Sax	musical instrument	
Louis Pasteur	process for killing germs	
Hamburg (a German city)	popular food	
General A.E. Burnside	facial hair	

Answers: Sax—saxophone, Pasteur—pasteurize or pasteurization, Hamburg—hamburger, Burnside—sideburns

Daily Vocabulary   Level 3

DAY	FOCUS WORD	ACTIVITIES	TEACHER'S NOTES
1	MATZO	Complete the following analogy: *Matzo* is to *bread* as *hammer* is to _____. matzo : bread :: hammer : _____	**Answer:** *tool* Matzo is a type of bread and a hammer is a type of tool. Matzo is thin and flat because it is made without yeast, which makes dough rise. Matzo is associated with the Jewish festival of Passover, celebrated each spring. According to legend, when the biblical Jews were freed from slavery, they left Egypt at once and did not even allow their bread dough to rise.
2	CHOWDER	Which word does not belong with the others? Tell why it does not belong. soup broth chowder casserole	**Answer:** *casserole*; it is not a type of soup. The focus word *chowder* means "a soup or stew made of fish, clams, or a vegetable, usually simmered in milk." This dish originated in France. **Reinforcement Activity:** Have students complete this analogy: *Clam* is to *chowder* as _____ is to *salad*. **Possible Answers:** *lettuce, tomato, broccoli*
3	SALSA	Unscramble the letters to make a word that names a dip for tortilla chips. LASAS	**Answer:** *salsa* The focus word *salsa* means "a spicy tomato and pepper sauce, usually red or green." You might ask students to name other Hispanic foods they like, such as *arroz con pollo, enchiladas suizas,* tacos, and tamales.

DAY	FOCUS WORD	ACTIVITIES	TEACHER'S NOTES
4	SUSHI	Which of the following is not an ingredient in sushi? **a.** fish **b.** salsa **c.** rice cakes **d.** seaweed	**Answer:** *b. salsa* The focus word *sushi* means "small cakes of cooked rice wrapped in seaweed, dressed in vinegar, and topped with slices of raw fish, boiled egg, or vegetables." Sushi is a Japanese dish.
5	SAUERKRAUT	Match the food with the culture. sushi German matzo Japanese sauerkraut Jewish	**Answers:** sushi—Japanese; matzo—Jewish; sauerkraut—German The focus word *sauerkraut* means "chopped cabbage that is pickled in a salty solution." In the German language, *sauer* means "sour," and *kraut* means "cabbage." Tell students that this famous German dish was created to keep cabbage from spoiling. The salt pickles the cabbage.

OPTIONAL EXTENSION ACTIVITY

This week's lesson provides an opportunity to build vocabulary while fostering students' appreciation of different cultures. Invite groups of students who share an ethnic background to give an oral report to the class describing traditional foods in their culture and listing the foods' ingredients. Encourage students to use visual aids in their presentations, such as a chart like the one shown.

Culture	Food	Ingredients
Italian	lasagna	pasta ground meat cheese tomato sauce

Daily Vocabulary　　　Level **3**

DAY	FOCUS WORD	ACTIVITIES	TEACHER'S NOTES
1	VAULT	Give a synonym for the word *vaulted* in the following sentence. 　The gymnast ran toward the leather horse and vaulted over it.	**Possible Answers:** *jumped, leaped, bounced* The words *gymnast* and *over* provide context clues to the meaning of *vault*, which means "to leap with the aid of the hands or a pole." **Reinforcement Activity:** Ask students to name other pieces of equipment used by gymnasts. **Possible Answers:** parallel bars, rings, balance beam, mat
2	DRIBBLE	Which word does not belong with the others? Tell why it does not belong. 　dribble　basketball　backboard　touchdown	**Answer:** *touchdown*; it does not pertain to basketball. The focus word *dribble* means "to move a ball forward by bouncing (in basketball)." **Reinforcement Activity:** Have students tell how a coach might help a player dribble better. **Possible Answer:** by telling the player to let the ball come to the hand instead of slapping at it
3	PUNT	Complete the following analogy: 　*Dribble* is to *hand* as *punt* is to _____. 　dribble : hand :: punt : _____	**Answer:** *foot* The focus word *punt* means "to kick a ball dropped from the hands before it hits the ground." You dribble with your hand and punt with your foot. **Reinforcement Activity:** Ask students to identify the word that does not belong and to explain why. 　punt　kick　boot　throw **Answer:** *throw*; it is an action of the hand.

Daily Vocabulary

DAY	FOCUS WORD	ACTIVITIES	TEACHER'S NOTES
4	BUNT	Match the sport and the activity. baseball punt football dribble basketball bunt	**Answer:** baseball—bunt; football—punt; basketball—dribble *Bunt* means "to hit a baseball with a half swing so that it rolls slowly in front of home plate." **Reinforcement Activity:** Have students complete the chain. baseball ➜ _____ ➜ bunt ➜ _____ ➜ _____ **Possible Answers:** *batter, ball, home plate*
5	SERVE	Which of the following would not be served? **a.** a tennis ball **b.** a volleyball **c.** a basketball **d.** a "birdie," or shuttlecock	**Answer:** c. *a basketball* The focus word *serve* means "to hit a ball to an opponent to start play." Serving is a skill important in such games as tennis, volleyball, and badminton.

OPTIONAL EXTENSION ACTIVITY

Invite students to bring in sports equipment and demonstrate to the class the correct techniques for performing the skills suggested by the focus words for this week. Alternatively, students might bring to class photographs of others performing these skills or videotapes of themselves playing various sports.

DAY	FOCUS WORD	ACTIVITIES	TEACHER'S NOTES
1	**PASSPORT**	Which word or phrase can replace the underlined words in the following sentence? Before my brother could leave on his trip to Ghana, West Africa, he had to get a <u>travel permit</u>. **a.** password **b.** passport **c.** driver's license **d.** sticker	**Answer:** *b. passport* The focus word *passport* means "a document that allows a citizen to leave a country." **Reinforcement Activity:** Ask students what information a passport might contain. **Possible Answers:** the traveler's name and citizenship
2	**DEPARTURE** **ARRIVAL**	Which word does not belong with the others? Tell why it does not belong. departure exit arrival leaving	**Answer:** *arrival*; it does not refer to leaving. The words *departure* and *arrival* are opposite in meaning. *Departure* means "a going away." It is a synonym of the words *exit* and *leaving*. *Arrival* means "a coming to a place." **Reinforcement Activity:** Ask students to tell about departures and arrivals they have experienced.
3	**TOURIST**	Which one of the following would a tourist probably not be seen doing? **a.** asking for directions **b.** taking pictures **c.** studying a local map **d.** driving a taxicab	**Answer:** *d. driving a taxicab* The focus word *tourist* means "a person who travels for pleasure." Explain that a tourist might be seen riding in a taxicab but not driving a taxicab. **Reinforcement Activity:** Ask students to identify places they might like to visit as tourists.

Daily Vocabulary

Level 3

DAY	FOCUS WORD	ACTIVITIES	TEACHER'S NOTES
4	BROCHURE	Make a word chain by writing in each blank a word that connects to the word that comes before it. traveler ➡ brochure ➡ ____ ➡ ____ ➡ ____	**Possible Answers:** *Yellowstone National Park, Old Faithful, geyser* The word *brochure* means "a pamphlet or booklet that advertises something." Ask students what a travel brochure might include (photographs and descriptions of tourist attractions, information about tours). You may also wish to discuss where travel brochures are usually found (travel bureaus, hotels, motels).
5	SCHEDULE	Choose the word that best completes the sentence. To find out the time of arrival of the next train, I looked at my _____. **a.** passport **b.** watch **c.** schedule **d.** ticket	**Answer:** *c. schedule* The focus word *schedule* means "a list of times set aside for certain events." Explain that although a train ticket may include departure and arrival times for a single train, it does not include a schedule of all arrivals and departures.

OPTIONAL EXTENSION ACTIVITY

Have small groups of students work together to create stories about characters' trips to foreign countries. Students should include this week's focus words in their stories. Encourage students to make a travel brochure or a train schedule to accompany their stories. Allow time for groups to share their work.

DAY	FOCUS WORD	ACTIVITIES	TEACHER'S NOTES
1	SOUND BITE	Which word or phrase can replace the underlined words in the following sentence? On the radio, we heard a <u>brief statement</u> from the mayor's speech. **a.** word **b.** sound bite **c.** sound effect **d.** report	**Answer:** *b. sound bite* *Sound bite* means "a brief recorded statement." Explain that *sound effect* refers to a recorded sound—such as that of an animal, thunder, or traffic—not to recorded words. **Reinforcement Activity:** Have students imagine that sound bites from conversations in the school lunchroom will be broadcast on the radio. Ask them what those sound bites might be.
2	PAN	What two different meanings does *pan* have in the following sentences? In the Old West, prospectors would pan for gold. The spectacular beauty of the Grand Canyon made the camera operator decide to pan the area.	**Answer:** In the first sentence, *pan* means "to wash gravel in a pan, searching for gold." In the second sentence, *pan* means "to rotate a camera horizontally." Explain to students that panning provides a panoramic, or complete, view of a scene or of the movement of an object.
3	LAUGH TRACK	Which of the following would a television comedy show probably not include? **a.** comedians **b.** funny jokes **c.** sound bites **d.** a laugh track	**Answer:** *c. sound bites* The focus word *laugh track* means "recorded laughter that is added to the soundtrack of a television program." **Reinforcement Activity:** Ask students why a laugh track might be used for a comedy show. **Possible Answer:** to prompt audience laughter

Daily Vocabulary

Level 3

DAY	FOCUS WORD	ACTIVITIES	TEACHER'S NOTES
4	ZOOM	Choose the best word or words to complete the following sentence. The camera _____ the crowd to focus on the President. **a.** panned **b.** circled **c.** zoomed in on **d.** pulled back from	**Answer:** *c. zoomed in on* The focus word *zoom* means "to give the effect of moving away from or toward an object." Explain that *zoomed in* suggests an apparent movement toward the crowd. **Reinforcement Activity:** Ask students to name a device, other than a camera, that might have a zoom lens. **Possible Answer:** a telescope
5	CANNED	What two different meanings does the word *canned* have in the following sentences? There were no fresh fruits left, so we bought canned peaches. The television station showed a canned interview with the celebrity a few days after he died.	**Answer:** In the first sentence, the word *canned* means "stored in a can." In the second sentence, *canned* means "recorded to be broadcast later." **Reinforcement Activity:** Ask a student to point out and explain the context clue in the second sentence. **Answer:** The words "a few days after he died" indicate that the interview was prerecorded.

OPTIONAL EXTENSION ACTIVITY

Invite groups of students to create skits about the filming of scenes from their favorite television programs. Have each group include at least the following characters in its skit: actors, a director, and a camera operator. Encourage students to use this week's words in their skits.